BASKETBALL
FOR FUN AND FITNESS

Enslow Publishing
101 W. 23rd Street
Suite 240
New York, NY 10011
USA

enslow.com

Jeff Mapua

Published in 2020 by Enslow Publishing, LLC.
101 W. 23rd Street, Suite 240, New York, NY 10011

Library of Congress Cataloging-in-Publication Data

Names: Mapua, Jeff, author.
Title: Basketball for fun and fitness / Jeff Mapua.
Description: New York : Enslow Publishing, 2020 | Series: Sports for fun and fitness | Includes bibliographical references and index. | Audience: Grade K to 4.
Identifiers: LCCN 2019002974| ISBN 9781978513310 (library bound) | ISBN 9781978513297 (pbk.) | ISBN 9781978513303 (6 pack)
Subjects: LCSH: Basketball—Juvenile literature. | Physical fitness—Juvenile literature.
Classification: LCC GV885.1 .M365 2020 | DDC 796.323—dc23
LC record available at https://lccn.loc.gov/2019002974

Printed in the United States of America

To Our Readers: We have done our best to make sure all website addresses in this book were active and appropriate when we went to press. However, the author and the publisher have no control over and assume no liability for the material available on those websites or on any websites they may link to. Any comments or suggestions can be sent by email to customerservice@enslow.com.

Photo Credits: Cover, p. 1 (basketball players) Mike Kemp/Getty Images; cover and interior pages (balls and birdie) Lightspring/Shutterstock.com; p. 7 Joseph Sohm/ Shutterstock.com; p. 8 Rebecca Nelson/DigitalVision/ Getty Images; p. 10 Ivsanmas/ Shutterstock.com; p. 13 Sergey Novikov/ Alamy Stock Photo; p. 15 Zoonar RF/ Getty Images; p. 16 FatCamera/ E+/ Getty Images; p. 19 Joos Mind/The Image Bank/ Getty Images; p. 21 Richard Mackson/ Sports Illustrated/ Getty Images; p. 22 Brand X Pictures/Stockbyte/ Getty Images; p. 25 Ronnie Kaufman/Corbis/ Getty Images; p. 27 Wavebreakmedia/iStock/ Getty Images; p. 28 © iStockphoto.com/fcscafeine.

Contents

Introduction

Basketball is a team sport. Teammates must work together to win a game. One player can play really well with the help of teammates. Other times, a coach can lead a team to play better than it ever has before. One legendary moment saw one player lead a team to victory without even playing the whole game.

In 1970, the Los Angeles Lakers basketball team played the New York Knicks for the National Basketball Association (NBA) Championship. The two teams had to play a series of seven games, with the first one to reach four wins becoming the champion. The Knicks won the fifth game of the series to lead three games to two. But the win came at a great cost. The Knicks' best player was Willis Reed. Reed won the league's 1969–1970

Most Valuable Player (MVP) award and the MVP for the 1970 All-Star Game. Reed was truly the best player that season. But in game 5 of the championship series, Reed tore a muscle in his thigh.

The injury was so bad that he was unable to play in game 6. Without Reed playing for the Knicks, the Lakers went on to win the game. The Lakers and the Knicks were then tied with three games each. The seventh and final game would determine the ultimate winner of the NBA season with or without Reed. What happened next made sports history.

"I didn't want to have to look at myself in the mirror 20 years later and say I wished I had tried to play," Reed would later say. He decided to fight through his injury and pain and play for his teammates. Reed received medication to help with the pain in his leg. He then limped out onto the court to play twenty-seven minutes of the forty-eight–minute game. Reed's courage motivated his teammates and spurred them to victory.

CHAPTER 1

Tip-Off!

The game of basketball is simple. Two teams play against each other and try to score the most points. Basketball can be a fun, exciting, and healthy activity.

The Basics

Points in basketball are scored when a player throws or "shoots" the ball into their hoop or basket. This is called a **field goal**. Field goals are worth two points. There is a special line on the basketball floor or court called the three-point line. A player who shoots and makes a

Basketball can be played indoors or outdoors, but each court is set up with the same lines, telling players where they can shoot the ball from.

basket from behind this line is awarded three points. If a player is fouled while shooting, they are awarded two free throws (three throws if the foul came during a three-point shot). Players shoot free throws from behind another special line on the floor called the free-throw line. A free throw is worth one point.

Shooting the ball well takes practice. The more
you practice, the better you will get!

Shooting the ball requires arm strength. Players can
build arm muscles by practicing their shooting. People
also lift weights to help them shoot from areas far from
the basket.

Of course, not every shot goes into the basket. Even
the very best players miss about half of their shots.

The basket is attached to a backboard. When a shot is missed, the ball often bounces off the backboard and back onto the court. This is called a **rebound**. Teams fight for rebounds in order to control the ball and score.

Fighting for rebounds can be difficult. Players need the ability to jump high and stand their ground. Playing basketball builds stronger leg muscles. It also helps people with their balance.

JAMES NAISMITH AND THE PEACH BASKET

Dr. James Naismith was a physical education instructor at a college in Massachusetts during the winter of 1891. During a blizzard, students began to get restless waiting indoors. Dr. Naismith invented a game to help the students pass the time. He hung a pair of peach baskets high up in a gym, and students had to throw a ball into one of the baskets. The game of basketball was born.

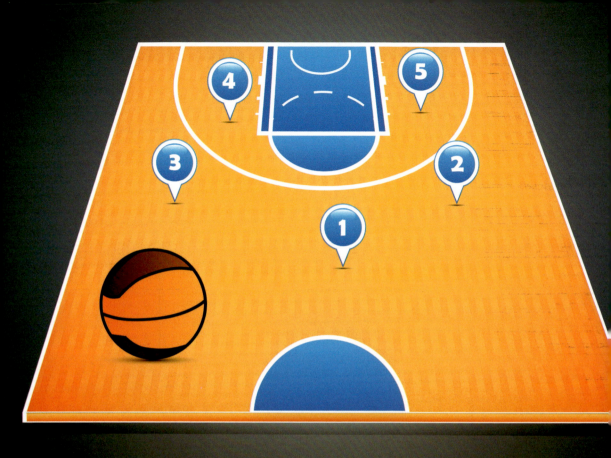

The positions in basketball are point guard (1), small forward (2), shooting guard (3), center (4), and power forward (5).

The ball is moved around the court by passing or dribbling. A player must **dribble**, or bounce, the ball with one hand while moving. The player must pass or shoot the ball once they stop dribbling.

Teams

Teams must have five players on the court at all times. Traditionally in basketball, the positions are called point guard, shooting guard, small forward, power forward, and center. The guards are usually smaller players with strengths in shooting, dribbling, and passing. Forwards are traditionally bigger than guards in order to better grab rebounds. Centers are usually the biggest players on the court in order to better stop the other team from scoring.

The team trying to score is on offense. A team trying to stop the other players from scoring is on defense. Players will have to switch between playing offense and defense during a game.

A game is divided into four quarters that usually last eight to twelve minutes each. There are short breaks between quarters to let players rest and drink water. There's a long break between the second and third quarters called halftime.

CHAPTER 2

Skills and Techniques

The game of basketball is simple, but there are many skills and techniques in the game. Practicing these skills can make someone a better player and teammate.

The Perfect Shot

Shooting is one of the most important skills in basketball. After all, teams need to make baskets to score points.

There are many kinds of shots in basketball. With a jump shot, your lower body can help you propel the ball into the basket.

Great shooting does more than score points, though. NBA players Stephen Curry and LeBron James are great shooters. They lift their teammates' spirits when they hit amazing shots.

There are many types of shots to practice. Each has a use in specific situations during a game. Players often jump when they shoot from long distance. This is called a jump shot. The extra power created from jumping helps get the ball to the basket. A layup is when a player runs and jumps toward the basket to shoot the ball from up close.

The best shooters practice shooting from many spots on the court. They practice free throws, jump shots, and three-pointers. Coaches tell their players to use the same shooting motion for all shots.

SLAM DUNK

One of the most exciting plays in basketball is the slam dunk. It begins when a player jumps into the air with the ball. The player then forces or slams it through the basket. Although it is the same number of points as a regular shot, people enjoy watching dunks more than most shots. There are even contests where people attempt **creative** dunks.

Slam dunks are even more powerful than jump shots.
Players run toward the basket and launch themselves
into the air, as close to the basket as possible!

When playing both offense and defense, running is important in basketball. Running can strengthen your legs for slam dunks.

Ball Handling

Great basketball players are able to control the ball in amazing ways. They dribble and move in any way they can imagine. Many NBA players have great **ball handling** skills. Some even have moves that earned nicknames such as "the killer crossover."

Players should practice dribbling with both hands. NBA Hall of Fame player Steve Nash practiced walking to school while dribbling with one hand. On his way home, he dribbled with his other hand. This helped develop his eye-hand coordination.

Defense

Not all skills are about scoring points. Defense is an important part of basketball. Many coaches believe that defense is more important than offense.

Defense is about staying between the offensive player and the basket. Players must have quick feet to keep up with an offensive player. Playing defense also means maintaining good balance.

While playing offense requires creativity, defense requires **determination**. Good defenders do not give up. They also help their teammates when they need it.

Fouls are called on defenders who get too physical with an offensive player. If a player collects too many fouls, they are no longer allowed to play in the game.

CHAPTER 3

Working as a Team

Basketball is a team sport. Skills can be practiced alone, but practicing how to play a game requires a team. In order to win, teammates must work together.

Offense

Teams on offense try to score points. Offensive players have the advantage over the defense because they know

Basketball skills can be practiced alone, but it is a team sport. In order to win, you have to learn how to work with your team.

what they will do next with the ball. Teams must move the ball up the court and into the basket. They do this by dribbling or passing to a teammate. Coaches tell their players to keep moving and passing until the ball goes to a teammate in position to score.

There are many different styles of basketball. Each style takes advantage of a team's strengths. Some teams play fast because they have fast players who shoot well. Other teams have big, strong players. Their style is to slow the game down and get the ball as close to the basket as possible.

Defense

Good team defenses have good communication skills. Teammates have to talk to each other on the court. For example, if a player is turned away from the ball, teammates tell the player what is happening behind them.

THE 1992 DREAM TEAM

In 1992, the United States sent a group of NBA players to the Olympics. The team featured players including legends Michael Jordan, Magic Johnson, and Larry Bird. Many believe it was the greatest team of all time. The team won the gold medal in a 117–85 win over Croatia. The team was very popular. Opposing teams would even try to get pictures with them during the game!

Playing defense can be tiring. Defenders have to work hard because they don't know what the offense will do next. Good defenders put pressure on the other team's offense. A defender tries to keep the player with the ball from going in the direction they want to go. Playing defense is a great way to get into good physical shape and build **endurance**.

Basketball isn't only played in your local park. In 1992, the Dream Team played in the Olympics and won the gold medal!

Good teams listen to their coach. A coach can help you
play your best with your fellow teammates.

Rebounding is considered a part of defense. Only when the defense controls the ball do players switch to playing offense. Teammates must work together to grab the basketball.

Listening to the Coach

Teammates must learn to work with one another to win. At the same time, players must be able to take directions from their coaches. That takes concentration and self-discipline. Coaches give players instructions and try to help bring the best out of the team. Basketball is also a great way to work on trusting others.

Good coaches teach good **sportsmanship** and respect toward teammates and other players. This is true for both wins and losses. Coaches also teach "we over me." One player cannot beat five opponents all on their own.

CHAPTER 4

More Games to Play

Basketball can be fun even without ten players on two teams playing on a full court. Over the years, people have invented fun **variations** or versions of basketball. These are perfect for when it is impossible to play a full game. All they take are a ball and a basketball hoop. You don't need ten players, but will still need to do these with some friends!

You don't need ten players to have fun with a basketball. You can play games in smaller groups, sharpening your skills for bigger games.

H-O-R-S-E

One of the most popular variations is H-O-R-S-E, or Horse. The game is a great way to practice shooting skills and technique. It can be played with two or more people.

The basic rules are simple. Players decide who goes first, second, and so on. The first person shoots from anywhere on the court. The more creative and difficult

HEALTHY ACTIVITIES

Healthy competition improves concentration and cooperation. Basketball does all that and more. It is considered an aerobic exercise. This means it helps strengthen a person's lungs and breathing. Playing also helps build muscle. Gaining strength and building muscle help avoid injury.

Basketball's fast-paced nature helps develop the brain, too. The game requires thinking quickly. People develop the ability to make quick decisions through playing.

the attempt the better. If they make the shot, the second person must attempt the same shot. If that person makes it, then the third person must also attempt the same shot. If the second person misses the shot, then they are given the letter H. The third person then attempts a shot from anywhere on the court they choose. Every time a person misses a shot the previous person makes, that player gets another letter until they spell "horse." The game ends when all but one player spells "horse."

Twenty-One

Twenty-One is an "every player for themselves" game. Each player tries to score a basket while the others all play defense. Field goals are worth two points each. Each made basket is followed by a free throw worth one point. If the basket is made, the player continues shooting free throws until one is missed. After three made free throws,

Practicing specific skills will help your game. Learning how to move the ball and your feet together will make you a great player.

27

Basketball is a fun way to learn about teamwork, but the game can also teach you about yourself!

the ball is put back into play. The game ends when one player scores twenty-one points.

The game is a fun way to learn how to play defense. It is also a good way to learn how to play against more than one defender at once. The game can be an intense physical activity, too.

There are many other basketball variations. These include Around the World and Knockout. Each focuses on a different basketball skill. Playing them can help people become even better basketball players and even better teammates.

Words to Know

ball handling   Skillful dribbling and accurate passing to control a basketball.

creative   Having original or imaginative ideas.

determination   Firm intention to do something, such as play defense.

dribble   To bounce the ball with one hand while walking, running, or standing still.

endurance   The ability to last or maintain constant physical activity.

field goal   When a player successfully shoots the ball into the basket.

rebound   To gain possession of the basketball after a missed shot bounces off the backboard or basket rim.

sportsmanship   Respect for opponents, fair play, and gracious winning and losing.

variation   A different version of something.

Learn More

Books

Kortemeier, Todd. *Fairness in Sports*. Lake Elmo, MN: Focus Readers, 2018.

Mableton, Barry, and Elizabeth Gettelman. *Basketball: Girls Rocking It.* New York, NY: Rosen Publishing, 2016.

Nagelhout, Ryan. *Basketball: Who Does What?* New York, NY: Gareth Stevens Publishing, 2018.

Small, Cathleen. *Basketball*. New York, NY: Gareth Stevens Publishing, 2019.

Websites

AVCSS Basketball

avcssbasketball.com/

This site is an online basketball resource that offers free basketball drills, plays, coaching tips, and information about the game.

Boys & Girls Clubs of America

bgca.org

Boys & Girls Clubs of America provide sports programs and clubs for kids of all ages.

Jr. NBA

jr.nba.com

Jr. NBA is a part of the National Basketball Association and encourages participation in basketball.

Index